Emergency
Arabic

Mahmoud Gaafar

Series Editor: Jane Wightwick
Art Director: Mark Wightwick

g-and-*W*

www.g-and-w.co.uk

Emergency

CONTENTS

Emergency

Arabic

Arabic

⚡TAKE NOTE⚡

Traveling to a country where the language and culture are unfamiliar is exciting but can also be challenging. Often a smile and good manners will carry you a long way, and it helps to learn how to say at least "please" and "thank you."

When things are going smoothly on your trip you'll probably not notice the communication difficulties that can arise from a language barrier. Many people speak some English and will be happy to practice on you. But in more stressful situations, especially in remoter areas, you cannot always rely on English to make yourself understood or to get you out of a jam.

Emergency Arabic is designed for these situations. Carry it with you and use it to explain your situation clearly and to make polite requests. There's a pronunciation guide to help you say the words and phrases, or you can show the book to Arabic-speakers so that they can read it in their own language. There are even special "Answer Back" panels designed for them to point out an answer to your question.

So put **Emergency Arabic** in your pocket and travel light with confidence!

basics

KEY WORDS

yes	نعم ◆ na'am
no	لا ◆ laa
please	من فضلك ◆ min faDlak
thank you	شكرا ◆ shukran
hello	أهلا ◆ ahlan
goodbye	مع السلامة ◆ ma'as-salaama
where?	أين؟ ◆ aina
here	هنا ◆ huna
when?	متى؟ ◆ mataa
now	الآن ◆ al-aan
tomorrow	غداً ◆ ghadan
how much?	بكم؟ ◆ bikam
I don't understand	لا أفهم ◆ laa afham

Down to

My name's...	...اسمي ◇ *ismee*
What's your name?	ما اسمك؟ ◇ *maa ismak*
Pleased to meet you	تشرفنا ◇ *tashar-rafna*
Where are you from?	أنت من أين؟ ◇ *anta min ain*
I'm American *(fem.)*	أنا أمريكي ◇ *ana amreekeyy(a)*
I'm English *(fem.)*	أنا انجليزي ◇ *ana ingleezeyy(a)*
I'm Canadian *(fem.)*	أنا كندي ◇ *ana kanadeyy(a)*
I'm Scottish *(fem.)*	أنا اسكتلندي ◇ *ana eskotlandeyy(a)*

Down to

basics

I'm Irish *(fem.)*	أنا ايرلندي ◆ *ana eerlandeyy(a)*
I'm Welsh *(fem.)*	أنا ويلزي ◆ *ana wilzeyy(a)*
I'm Australian *(fem.)*	أنا أسترالي ◆ *ana ostoraaleyy(a)*
I now live in...	الآن أعيش في... ◆ *al-aan a'eesh fee*

please point here ... أشر هنا من فضلك

أنا اسمي...	My name's...
أنا مصري	I'm Egyptian
أنا سوري	I'm Syrian
أنا مغربي	I'm Moroccan
أنا يمني	I'm Yemeni
أنا فلسطيني	I'm Palestinian

please point here ... أشر هنا من فضلك

basics

my husband	زوجي ◇ *zawjee*
my wife	زوجتي ◇ *zawjatee*
my son	ابني ◇ *ibnee*
my daughter	ابنتي ◇ *ibnatee*
my mother	أمي ◇ *um-mee*
my father	أبي ◇ *abee*
my sister	أختي ◇ *ukh-tee*
my brother	أخي ◇ *akhee*
my father-in-law/ my mother-in-law	حماي / حماتي ◇ *Hamaaya/ Hamaatee*
my daughter-in-law/ my son-in-law	زوجة ابني / زوج بنتي ◇ *zawjat ibnee/ zawj bintee*
my family	أسرتي ◇ *osratee*
my relatives	أقربائي ◇ *aqribaa'ee*
my friend (masc.)/ fiancé	صديقي /خطيبي ◇ *Sadeeqee/khaTeebee*
my friend (fem.)/ fiancée	صديقتي /خطيبتي ◇ *Sadeeqatee/khaTeebatee*

basics

He is my partner/ She is my partner	هو شريكي /هي شريكتي ◆ *huwa shareekee/* *hiya shareekatee*
I have two daughters	عندي ابنتين ◆ *ana 'indee ibnatain*
I have two sons	عندي ولدين ◆ *'indee waladain*
My mother is here with us	أمي معنا هنا ◆ *ummee ma'na huna*

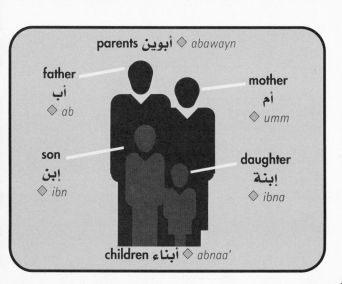

parents **أبوين** ◆ *abawayn*

father
أب
◆ *ab*

mother
أم
◆ *umm*

son
إبن
◆ *ibn*

daughter
إبنة
◆ *ibna*

children **أبناء** ◆ *abnaa'*

KEY WORDS

bathroom	حمّام ◈ *Ham-maam*
bedroom	غرفة نوم ◈ *ghorfat nawm*
hot water	ماء ساخن ◈ *maa' saakhin*
toilet	تواليت ◈ *tuwaaleet*
sink	حوض ◈ *HawD*
faucet (tap)	صنبور ◈ *Sunboor*
drain	بالوعة ◈ *baaloo'a*
shower	دُش ◈ *dosh-sh*
bathtub	بانيو ◈ *banyo*
soap	صابون ◈ *Saaboon*
towel	منشفة ◈ *minshafa*
key	مفتاح ◈ *miftaaH*
lock	قفل ◈ *qifl*

to stay

door	باب ◈ *baab*
chair	كرسي ◈ *korseyy*
table	مائدة ◈ *maa'ida*
television	تليفزيون ◈ *telivizyoon*
light	نور ◈ *noor*
curtain	ستار ◈ *setaar*
bed	سرير ◈ *sareer*
blanket	بطانية ◈ *baT-Taaneyya*
pillow	وسادة ◈ *wesaada*
heater	مدفأة ◈ *midfa'ah*
air-conditioning	تكييف هواء ◈ *takyeef hawaa'*
crib (cot)	سرير أطفال ◈ *sareer aTfaal*
highchair	كرسي أطفال ◈ *korseyy aTfaal*

to stay

An extra blanket, please	بطانية إضافية من فضلك
	◇ baT-Taaneyya iDaafeyya, min faDlak
Put the crib (cot) over there	ضع سرير الأطفال هناك
	◇ Da' sareer al-aTfaal hunaak
We need soap and towels	نحتاج صابون ومناشف
	◇ naHtaaj Saaboon wa manaashif
The air-conditioning doesn't work	تكييف الهواء لا يعمل
	◇ takyeef al-hawaa' laa ya'mal
Can you repair the toilet?	ممكن تصلح التواليت ؟
	◇ momkin teSal-laH at-tuwaaleet
There's no hot water	لا يوجد ماء ساخن
	◇ laa yawjad maa' saakhin
too hot/too cold	ساخنة جدا / باردة جدا
	◇ saakhina jid-dan/ baarida jid-dan

to stay

The window is jammed shut	الشباك محشور لا يفتح
	◆ ash-shubbaak maHshoor laa yaftaH
My key is lost	مفتاحي ضاع
	◆ miftaaHee Daa'
How do we open this door?	كيف نفتح هذا الباب؟
	◆ kaifa naftaH haazal baab

please point here ... أشر هنا من فضلك ...

سنصلحه فورا	We'll repair it right away
سيأتي شخص ليساعدك	Someone will come to help you
سنحضره إلى غرفتكم	We'll bring it to your room
اتركها مع البواب	Leave them with the doorman
من فضلك اسأل الاستقبال	Please ask reception

please point here ...

A place

RENTING

kitchen	مطبخ ◆ maTbakh
living room	غرفة جلوس ◆ ghorfat joloos
dining room	غرفة طعام ◆ ghorfat Ta'aam
garbage	زبالة ◆ zebaala
electric meter	عداد ◆ 'ad-daad
deposit	تأمين ◆ ta'meen
inventory	قائمة ◆ qaa'ima
Where will we find the key?	أين سنجد المفتاح؟ ◆ aina sa-najid al-miftaaH

⚡TAKE NOTE⚡

Most rentals are long term. Short-term visitors will generally use hotels. In some resorts, however, you may rent a bungalow, a chalet, or an apartment.

A place

to stay

Where do we leave the garbage?	أين نترك الزبالة؟ ◆ aina natrok az-zebaala
Where are the sheets/towels?	أين الملايات/المناشف؟ ◆ ainal milaayaat/ manaashif
How much is the deposit?	كم قيمة التأمين؟ ◆ kam qeemat at-ta'meen
Will we pay for cleaning?	هل سندفع التنظيف؟ ◆ hal sa-nadfa' at-tanZeef

please point here ... أشر هنا من فضلك

المفاتيح في الاستقبال	The keys are at reception
سنقابلكم هناك	We'll meet you there
هذا سعره إضافي	You have to pay extra for that

أشر هنا من فضلك ... please point here

PAYMENT

I'll need an invoice	سأحتاج فاتورة ◆ sa-aHtaaj fatoora
The invoice has a mistake	هناك خطأ في الفاتورة ◆ hunaak khaTa' fil fatoora
We didn't take this	لم نأخذ هذا ◆ lam na'khoz haaza
We only took one/two	أخذنا واحدة/اثنان فقط ◆ akhazna waaHida/ ithnaan faqaT
We didn't use the telephone	لم نستعمل التليفون ◆ lam nasta'mil at-telifoon
We didn't break this	لم نكسر هذا ◆ lam naksar haaza
We've paid for it	دفعنا ثمنه ◆ dafa'na thamanuh
Is the manager available?	المدير موجود؟ ◆ al-modeer mawjood

The total would be...	الإجمالي يكون...
	◆ al-ijmaalee yakoon

Is this card acceptable?	هل هذا الكارت مقبول؟
	◆ hal haazal kart maqbool

We only have traveler's checks.	معنا شيكات سياحية فقط
	◆ ma'naa sheekaat siyaaHeyya faqaT

➡ **Page 47 for Numbers**

please point here ... أشر هنا من فضلك ...

دعني أسأل في الداخل	Let me ask inside
سنصلحها	We'll correct it
الفاتورة سليمة الآن	The invoice is correct now
خصمناه من التأمين	We deducted it from the deposit
لحظة، سأنادي المدير	One moment, I'll call the manager

please point here ...

KEY WORDS

map	خريطة ◇ khareeTa
address	عنوان ◇ 'unwaan
street	شارع ◇ shaari'
highway	طريق سريع ◇ Tareeq saree'
distance	مسافة ◇ masaafa
meter	متر ◇ mitr
kilometer	كيلومتر ◇ kilomitr
sign	علامة ◇ 'alaama
direction	اتجاه ◇ it-tijaah
right	يمين ◇ yameen
left	يسار ◇ yasaar
straight on	على طول ◇ 'ala Tool
junction	تقاطع ◇ taqaaTo'

Excuse me

we're lost!

corner	ناصية ◈ naaSiya
traffic light	إشارة مرور ◈ ishaarat moroor
traffic circle (roundabout)	دوران ◈ dawaraan
desert road	طريق صحراوي ◈ Tareeq SaHraaweyy
on foot	مشي ◈ masheyy
by car	بالسيارة ◈ bis-sayyaara
by bus	بالباص ◈ bil-baaS
by train	بالقطار ◈ bil-qiTaar
by boat/ferry	بالمركب/بالمعدية ◈ bil-markib/ bil me'ad-deyya
by plane	بالطائرة ◈ biT-Taa'ira

we're lost!

Excuse me

Excuse me!	**لو سمحت!** ◆ lau samaHt
Where's …?	**أين...؟** ◆ aina
What street is this?	**أي شارع هذا؟** ◆ ayy shaari' haaza
What building is this?	**أي مبنى هذا؟** ◆ ayy mabna haaza
Where are we on the map?	**أين نحن على الخريطة؟** ◆ aina naHnu 'alal khareeTa
Which is the way there?	**أين الطريق إلى هناك؟** ◆ aina T-Tareeq ila hunaak
Is it far?	**هل هي بعيدة؟** ◆ hal hiya ba'eeda
Which is the easiest way?	**ما هي أسهل طريقة؟** ◆ maa hiya as-hal Tareeqa

Excuse me

we're lost!

سأدلكم على طريق سهل	I'll show you an easy way
إنها قريبة	It's close
إنها بعيدة	It's far
خذوا الباص	Take the bus
خذوا تاكسي أفضل	Better take a taxi
اتجه إلى اليمين	Turn right
اتجه إلى اليسار	Turn left
أول /ثاني /ثالث شارع	First/second/ third street
على طول	Straight on
بعد أن تعبر...	After you cross...
اترك...	Go past...
أمام...	Opposite...

➡ Page 24 for landmarks

we're lost!

21

Excuse me

I'm a visitor	أنا زائر ◈ *ana zaa'ir*
I didn't know it was one-way	لم أعرف أنه اتجاه واحد ◈ *lam a'rif an-nu it-tijaah waaHid*
I don't read Arabic signs	أنا لا أقرأ لافتات بالعربية ◈ *ana laa aqra' lafitaat bil 'arabey-ya*
How much is the fine?	كم الغرامة؟ ◈ *kam al-gharaama*
Can I leave the car here?	ممكن أترك السيارة هنا؟ ◈ *momkin atrok as-say-yaara hona*

⚡TAKE NOTE⚡

Because they have foreigners in mind, traffic authorities will often erect street signs in both Arabic and English. If you're driving, try not to get distracted by funny spelling mistakes!

Broadly speaking, try always to expect the unexpected. The element of surprise keeps everyone on their toes. Honking is almost an involuntary activity, so don't take it too personally. It is not as forceful a statement as it may be in Europe or the US.

Excuse me

we're lost!

TRAFFIC INSTRUCTIONS

no entry	ممنوع الدخول ◇ *mamnoo' ad-dokhool*
no parking	ممنوع الانتظار ◇ *mamnoo' lintiZaar*
stop!	قف! ◇ *qiff*
slow down!	هدئ السرعة! ◇ *had-di' as-sor'a*
keep right!	الزم اليمين! ◇ *ilzam al-yameen*
keep left!	الزم اليسار! ◇ *ilzam al-yasaar*
pedestrians only	للمشاه فقط ◇ *lil-moshaah faqaT*
buses only	للباصات فقط ◇ *lil-baaSaat faqaT*
bicycle path	ممر للدراجات ◇ *mamarr lid-dar-raajaat*
crossing	عبور ◇ *'uboor*

we're lost!

LANDMARKS

airport	مطار ◇ *maTaar*
bank	بنك ◇ *bank*
beach	شاطئ ◇ *shaaTi'*
bridge	جسر ◇ *jisr*
bus stop	موقف باصات ◇ *mawqaf baSaat*
campsite	مخيم ◇ *mokhay-yam*
castle	قلعة ◇ *qal'a*
cave	كهف ◇ *kahf*
temple	معبد ◇ *ma'bad*
palace	قصر ◇ *qaSr*
river	نهر ◇ *nahr*
youth hostel	بيت الشباب ◇ *bait ash-shabaab*

Excuse me

we're lost!

hotel	فندق ◆ *funduq*
lake	بحيرة ◆ *boHaira*
mountain	جبل ◆ *jabal*
theater	مسرح ◆ *masraH*
museum	متحف ◆ *matHaf*
park	حديقة ◆ *Hadeeqa*
parking lot (car park)	موقف سيارات ◆ *mawqaf say-yaaraat*
school	مدرسة ◆ *madrasa*
square	ميدان ◆ *meedaan*
station	محطة ◆ *maHaT-Ta*
mosque	مسجد ◆ *masjid*
statue	تمثال ◆ *timthaal*
market	سوق ◆ *sooq*
university	جامعة ◆ *jaami'a*

KEY WORDS

appointment	موعد ◈ *maw'id*
doctor	دكتور ◈ *doktoor*
dentist	دكتور أسنان ◈ *doktoor asnaan*
nurse	ممرضة ◈ *momar-reDa*
ambulance	إسعاف ◈ *is'aaf*
hospital	مستشفى ◈ *mostashfa*
clinic	عيادة ◈ *'iyaada*
ward	عنبر ◈ *'anbar*
stretcher	نقالة ◈ *naq-qaala*
operation	جراحة ◈ *jiraaHa*
injury	إصابة ◈ *iSaaba*
illness	مرض ◈ *maraD*
insurance	تأمين ◈ *ta'meen*

doctor!

examination	◆ فحص	faHS
test	◆ اختبار	ikhtibaar
prescription	◆ روشتة	roshet-ta
pharmacy	◆ صيدلية	Saydaley-ya
medicine	◆ دواء	dawaa'
pill	◆ حبة	Hab-ba
injection	◆ حقنة	Hoqna
syrup	◆ شراب	sharaab
ointment	◆ مرهم	marham
suppository	◆ لبوس	loboos
painkiller	◆ مسكن	mosak-kin
sedative	◆ مهدئ	mohad-di'
analysis	◆ تحليل	taHleel
x-ray	◆ أشعة	ashi'a

doctor!

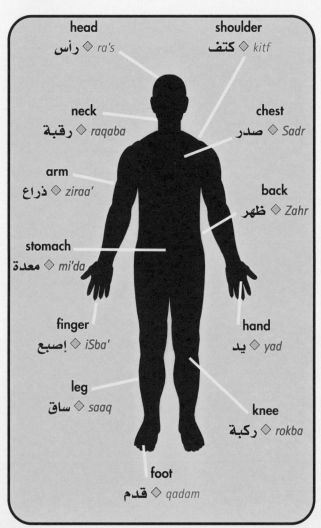

head
◇ *ra's* رأس

shoulder
◇ *kitf* كتف

neck
◇ *raqaba* رقبة

chest
◇ *Sadr* صدر

arm
◇ *ziraa'* ذراع

back
◇ *Zahr* ظهر

stomach
◇ *mi'da* معدة

finger
◇ *iSba'* إصبع

hand
◇ *yad* يد

leg
◇ *saaq* ساق

knee
◇ *rokba* ركبة

foot
◇ *qadam* قدم

doctor!

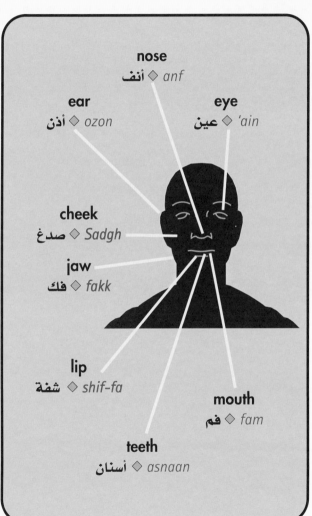

nose
أنف ◇ *anf*

ear
أذن ◇ *ozon*

eye
عين ◇ *'ain*

cheek
صدغ ◇ *Sadgh*

jaw
فك ◇ *fakk*

lip
شفة ◇ *shif-fa*

mouth
فم ◇ *fam*

teeth
أسنان ◇ *asnaan*

The pain is here	الألم هنا
	◆ *al-alam huna*
I can't move it	لا يمكنني أن أحركه
	◆ *laa yomkinonee an uHar-rikkuh*
I have a headache	عندي صداع
	◆ *'indee Sodaa'*
I have a stomachache	عندي مغص
	◆ *'indee maghaS*
My back hurts	عندي ألم في ظهري
	◆ *'indee alam fee Zahree*
I feel sick	أشعر بالغثيان ◆ *ash'or bil-ghathayaan*
I have diarrhea	عندي إسهال
	◆ *'indee is-haal*

doctor!

استلق هنا	Lie down here
افتح فمك	Open your mouth
خذ نفس عميق	Breathe deeply
اسعل	Cough
ارفع هذا الكم	Roll up this sleeve
ارفع قميصك	Lift up your shirt
اثن ركبتيك	bend your knees

please point here ... أشر هنا من فضلك

⚡ TAKE NOTE ⚡

An accurate diagnosis may depend on the clarity and precision of what you say, and the ability of the doctor to understand exactly what you mean.

doctor!

Is it serious?	هل الأمر خطير؟
	◇ hal al-amr khaTeer
Is it infectious?	هل هو معد؟
	◇ hal huwa mo'di
Can it wait?	هل يمكنه الانتظار؟
	◇ hal yumkinuh al-intiZaar
I'll call our family doctor	سأتصل بطبيب العائلة
	◇ sa'at-taSil bi-Tabeeb al-'aa'ila
Where's the nearest pharmacy?	أين أقرب صيدلية؟
	◇ aina aqrab Saydaley-ya
I will contact my insurer	سأتصل بشركة التأمين
	◇ sa'at-taSil bi-sherikat at-ta'meen
I'm not insured	ليس عندي تأمين
	◇ laisa 'indee ta'meen
Can I have a receipt?	ممكن تعطيني ايصال؟
	◇ momkin tu'Teenee eeSaal

doctor!

هل أنت مريض بالسكري؟	Are you diabetic?
إنها من أعراض ضربة الشمس	It's a symptom of sunstroke
عندك التهاب بسيط	You have a minor infection
أنا غير متأكد الآن	I'm not sure yet
أحتاج أن أراك مرة أخرى غدا	I need to see you again tomorrow
يجب أن تذهب إلى المستشفى	You have to go to the hospital
لا تتعرض للشمس	Keep out of the sun
اشرب ماء كثير	Drink plenty of water
خذ هذا الدواء	Take this medicine
قبل /بعد الوجبات	before/after meals
هل عندك حساسية؟	Are you allergic to anything?

There's been

KEY WORDS

car	سيارة ◇ *say-yaara*
motorbike	دراجة نارية ◇ *dar-raaja naarey-ya*
bicycle	دراجة ◇ *dar-raaja*
boat	مركب ◇ *markib*
truck (lorry)	شاحنة ◇ *shaaHina*
donkey	حمار ◇ *Himaar*
driver	سائق ◇ *saa'iq*
bus	باص ◇ *baaS*
pedestrians	مشاه ◇ *moshaah*
child	طفل ◇ *Tifl*
dog	كلب ◇ *kalb*

There's been

brakes	مكابح ◇ *makaabiH*
animal	حيوان ◇ *Haywaan*
tree	شجرة ◇ *shajara*
ditch	حفرة ◇ *Hofra*
curve	منحنى ◇ *monHana*
flood	فيضان ◇ *fayaDaan*
cell phone (mobile phone)	تليفون محمول ◇ *telifoon maHmool*
public telephone	تليفون عام ◇ *telifoon 'aam*
police	شرطة ◇ *shorTa*
ambulance	إسعاف ◇ *is'aaf*
fire engine	مطافي ◇ *maTaafee*
rescue	إنقاذ ◇ *inqaaz*
witness	شاهد ◇ *shaahid*

| Come quickly! | تعال بسرعة! |
| | ◇ ta'ala bi-sor'a |

| Someone is hurt | يوجد شخص مصاب |
| | ◇ yewjad shakhS moSaab |

| Call an ambulance! | اطلب الإسعاف! |
| | ◇ oTlob al-is'aaf |

| Where's a telephone? | أين التليفون؟ |
| | ◇ ain at-telifoon |

| Don't move him | لا تحركه |
| | ◇ laa toHar-rikuh |

| It wasn't our fault | لم تكن غلطتنا |
| | ◇ lam takun ghalTatna |

| They saw everything | هم شاهدوا كل شئ |
| | ◇ hom shaahadu koll shai' |

| first aid | اسعافات أولية |
| | ◇ is'aafaat aw-waley-ya |

There's been

an accident!

please point here ... أشر هنا من فضلك

أين وقع الحادث؟	Where did it happen?
هل رآه أحد؟	Did anyone see it?
يجب أن نبلغ عنه	We need to report it
رخصتك من فضلك	Your license, please
التأمين من فضلك	The insurance, please

please point here ... أشر هنا من فضلك

⚡TAKE NOTE⚡

Accidents are no fun anywhere in the world. All you can realistically be expected to do is prepare yourself as best you can by carrying a fire extinguisher, a first-aid box and a red reflective triangle. Try to keep a cool, clear head, stay at the scene and wait for the police.

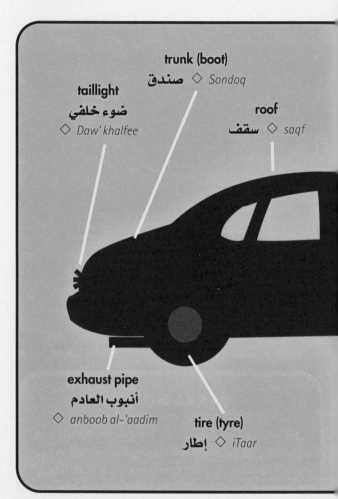

trunk (boot)
صندق ◇ *Sondoq*

taillight
ضوء خلفي
◇ *Daw' khalfee*

roof
سقف ◇ *saqf*

exhaust pipe
أنبوب العادم
◇ *anboob al-'aadim*

tire (tyre)
إطار ◇ *iTaar*

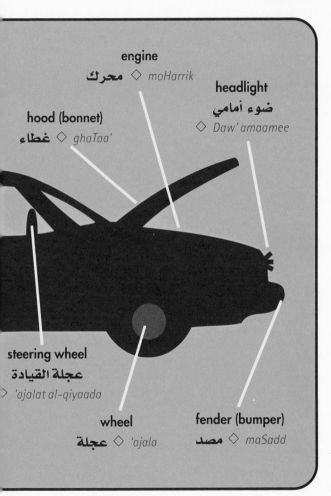

engine
محرك ◇ *moHarrik*

headlight
ضوء أمامي
◇ *Daw' amaamee*

hood (bonnet)
غطاء ◇ *ghaTaa'*

steering wheel
عجلة القيادة
◇ *'ajalat al-qiyaada*

wheel
عجلة ◇ *'ajala*

fender (bumper)
مصد ◇ *maSadd*

There's something wrong with it	هناك عطل فيها ◈ *hunaak 'oTl feehaa*
The exhaust pipe is too loud	أنبوب العادم مزعج ◈ *onboob al-'aadim muz'ij*
It's lost power	إنها بلا عزم ◈ *in-nahaa bilaa 'azm*
The engine won't start	المحرك لا يدور ◈ *al-muHar-rik laa yadoor*
The oil is leaking	الزيت يتسرب ◈ *az-zait yatasar-rab*
It's overheating	إنها تسخن جدا ◈ *in-nahaa taskhan jid-dan*
Can you repair it?	ممكن تصلحها؟ ◈ *momkin tuSaliH-haa*

There's been

How long will it take?	كم تستغرق من الوقت؟ ◆ kam tastaghriq min al-waqt
What's the cost?	كم التكلفة؟ ◆ kam at-taklifa

أنا ممكن أصلحها	I can repair it
ستكون جاهزة اليوم	It'll be ready today
ستكون جاهزة غدا	It'll be ready tomorrow
سأطلب قطعة الغيار	I'll order the part
لا يمكن تصليحها	It can't be repaired
ستتكلف…	It will cost…
على ضمانتي	I guarantee it

Money

KEY WORDS

savings account	حساب إدخار ◇ *Hisaab id-dikhaar*
current account	حساب جار ◇ *Hisaab jaari*
ATM (cash machine)	جهاز صرف تلقائي ◇ *jihaaz Sarf tilqaa'eyy*
bank	بنك ◇ *bank*
bill (note)	بنكنوت ◇ *bankenoot*
cash	نقدا ◇ *naqdan*
check (cheque)	شيك ◇ *sheek*
coin	عملة معدنية ◇ *'omla ma'daneyya*
commission	عمولة ◇ *'omoola*
credit card	بطاقة ائتمان ◇ *biTaaqat i'timaan*

Money

talk

currency exchange	تغيير عملة ◆ taghyeer 'omla
exchange rate	سعر صرف ◆ si'r Sarf
form	استمارة ◆ istimaara
ID	تحقيق شخصية ◆ taHqeeq shakhSey-ya
money	مال ◆ maal
pin number	رقم سري ◆ raqam sir-reyy
signature	توقيع ◆ tawqee'
small change	فكة ◆ fak-ka
teller (cashier)	صرّاف ◆ Sar-raaf
transfer	تحويل ◆ taHweel
traveler's checks (traveller's cheques)	◆ شيكات سياحية sheekaat seyaaHey-ya
withdrawal	سحب ◆ SaHb

talk

I'd like to change...	أود أن أغيير...
	◈ awad an ughay-yir
What's the exchange rate?	ما هو سعر الصرف؟
	◈ maa huwa si'r aS-Sarf
I need to make a transfer	أود أن أقوم بتحويل
	◈ awad an aqoom bi-taHweel
How long will it take?	كم من الوقت يستغرق؟
	◈ kam min al-waqt yastaghriq
The machine won't accept it	الجهاز لا يقبله
	◈ aj-jihaaz laa yaqbaluh

talk

The ATM has eaten my card	الجهاز التهم بطاقتي ◆ *aj-jihaaz iltaham bi-Taaqatee*
I've forgotten my pin number	نسيت رقمي السري ◆ *naseet raqamee as-sirreyy*

please point here ... أشر هنا من فضلك ...

سأحتاج أن أرى جواز سفرك	I'll need to see your passport
ما هو رقم الحساب؟	What's the account number?
إذهب إلى شباك رقم...	Go to window number...
الإسم هنا مختلف	The name here is different
هذا ليس نفس التوقيع	This isn't the same signature

please point here ...

talk

Money

SETTLING UP

check (bill)	الفاتورة ◆ al-fatoora
service charge	أجر الخدمة ◆ ajr al-khidma
sales tax	ضريبة المبيعات ◆ Dareebat al-mabee'aat
cover charge	كوفير ◆ koofair
tip	إكرامية ◆ ikraamey-ya
receipt	إيصال ◆ eeSaal
How much is this?	بكم هذا؟ ◆ bikam haaza
Is service included?	هل يشمل الخدمة؟ ◆ hal yashmal al-khidma
Is tax included?	هل يشمل الضريبة؟ ◆ hal yashmal aD-Dareeba

Money

talk

A receipt, please	إيصال من فضلك
	◈ *eeSaal min faDlak*

Keep the change	احتفظ بالباقي
	◈ *iHtafiZ bil-baaqi*

⚡TAKE NOTE⚡

A 10% tip is normal in a restaurant, unless you are particularly pleased, in which case you may leave more.

The principal is the same for taxi-drivers, tour guides, and similar locally-provided services.

Most upmarket restaurants and hotels will accept credit cards and include tax and service in the price. The numbers are likely to be printed in English.

In a more 'back-alley' place, you may wish to check beforehand whether it is a cash-only establishment.

Money

What's this amount for?	لم هذا المبلغ؟ ◇ lima haazal mablagh
The total isn't right	هناك خطأ في الإجمالي ◇ hunaak khaTa' fil-ijmaalee
That's too expensive	هذا غال جدا ◇ haaza ghaali jid-dan
I want to exchange this	أريد استبدال هذا ◇ oreed istibdaal haaza
I want a refund	أريد استرجاع نقودي ◇ oreed istirjaa' noqoodee
I want to see the manager	أريد أن أقابل المدير ◇ oreed an oqaabil al-modeer
I don't have another card	ليس معي بطاقة أخرى ◇ laisa ma'ee biTaaqa okhra

Money

talk

I've forgotten
my wallet

نسيت حافظة نقودي
◆ naseet HaafiZat
noqoodee

أحتاج إلى طبعة من بطاقة الائتمان	I need an imprint of the credit card
لا نتعامل ببطاقات الائتمان	We don't accept credit cards
إذهب إلى الصرّاف	Go to the cashier
لا نتعامل بهذه البطاقة	We don't accept this card
سأعطيك فاتورة مفصلة	I'll give you an itemised invoice

➤ Page 16–17 for hotel/accommodation

talk

49

KEY WORDS

allergy	◇ *Hasaaseyya* حساسية
calories	سعرات حرارية ◇ *si'raat Haraareyya*
diabetic	مريض بالسكري ◇ *mareeD bis-sok-kareyy*
diet	نظام تغذية ◇ *niZaam taghzey-ya*
fat	◇ *dihn* دهن
food poisoning	◇ *tasam-mom* تسمم
halal	◇ *Halaal* حلال
ingredients	مكونات ◇ *mokaw-winaat*
intolerance to...	لا يتقبل... ◇ *laa yataqab-bal*
kosher	مباح لليهود ◇ *mobaaH lil-yahood*

salt	ملح ◆ malH
sugar	سكر ◆ sok-kar
vegetarian	نباتي ◆ nabaateyy

⚡TAKE NOTE⚡

Lamb and chicken are probably the most popular meats in the Middle East. A vegetarian from a western country remains largely a novelty. But vegans are so unknown that the word doesn't even exist in the Arabic dictionaries.

Typically, Middle Eastern cuisine has no particular hang-ups about lashings of salt, bundles of white sugar, dollops of ghee, gallons of full-fat milk, or sacks of bleached white flour. It's where it all leads to that matters: dishes so delicious you have to have some more (and maybe diet it off when you get back home.)

To be fair, you can also buy lots of healthy, organic and unprocessed foods where you can taste the goodness.

# I'm allergic

I have an allergy	عندي حساسية	◆ 'indee Hasaaseyya
I don't eat...	لا آكل ...	◆ laa aakol
I don't like...	لا أحب ...	◆ laa oHibb

➡ **Page 54–57 for types of food**

I'm vegetarian	أنا نباتي	◆ anaa nabaateyy
I'm diabetic	أنا مريض بالسكري	◆ anaa mareeD bis-sok-kareyy
What meat is this?	أي نوع لحم هذا؟	◆ ayy naw' laHm haaza
Does this contain nuts?	هل يحتوي على مكسرات؟	◆ hal yaHtawee 'ala mekas-saraat
Does this contain wheat?	هل يحتوي على قمح؟	◆ hal yaHtawi 'ala qamH
Are you sure?	هل أنت واثق؟	◆ hal anta waathiq

I'm allergic

to seafood!

Can we check with the chef?	ممكن نتأكد من الطباخ؟	◆ *mumkin nit'ak-kid min aT-Tabaakh*
The children always ask for it	الأطفال يطلبونه دائما	◆ *al-aTfaal yaTloboonuh daa'iman*

أشر هنا من فضلك ... **please point here ...**

ممكن نجهز طبق بدونه	We can prepare a dish without it
جرب هذا الطبق!	Try this dish!
آسف! لا يوجد شئ يناسبكم	Sorry, we have nothing suitable
دعني أسأل الطباخ	Let me ask the chef
أنا واثق أنه سيعجبكم	I'm sure you'll like it!
الأطفال لا يحبونه أبدا!	Kids never like it!

please point here ... أشر هنا من فضلك ...

I'm allergic

FOOD FINDER

apple	تفاح ◆	*tof-faaH*
banana	موز ◆	*mawz*
beef	لحم بقري ◆	*laHm baqareyy*
carrot	جزر ◆	*jazar*
chicken	دجاج ◆	*dajaaj*
chili	شطة ◆	*shaT-Ta*
corn	ذرة ◆	*dora*
cucumber	خيار ◆	*khiyaar*
duck	بط ◆	*baTT*
fish	سمك ◆	*samak*
garlic	ثوم ◆	*thawm*
ginger	جنزبيل ◆	*ganzabeel*
goat	لحم ماعز ◆	*laHm maa'iz*
kidney	كلاوي ◆	*kalaawi*
lamb	ضأن ◆	*Da'nee*
lemon	ليمون ◆	*laimoon*
lentil	عدس ◆	*'ads*
liver	كبدة ◆	*kibda*

I'm allergic

to seafood!

English–Arabic

mushrooms	فطر ◆ *fiTr*
nuts	مكسرات ◆ *mekas-saraat*
onion	بصل ◆ *baSal*
orange	برتقال ◆ *bortoqaal*
peanuts	**فول سوداني** ◆ *fool sudaaneyy*
pigeon	حمام ◆ *Hamaam*
potato	بطاطس ◆ *baTaaTis*
rabbit	أرانب ◆ *araanib*
rice	أرز ◆ *arozz*
seafood	**مأكولات بحرية** ◆ *ma'koolaat baHrey-ya*
shrimp (prawns)	جمبري ◆ *gambaree*
soybeans	**فول صويا** ◆ *fool Soya*
strawberries	فراولة ◆ *farawla*
thyme	زعتر ◆ *za'tar*
tomato	طماطم ◆ *TamaaTim*
veal	**لحم بتلو** ◆ *laHm bitel-lo*

to seafood!

FOOD FINDER

'ads	عدس	lentil
araanib	أرانب	rabbit
arozz	أرز	rice
baSal	بصل	onion
baTaaTis	بطاطس	potato
baTT	بط	duck
bortoqaal	برتقال	orange
Da'nee	ضأن	lamb
dajaaj	دجاج	chicken
farawla	فراولة	strawberries
fiTr	فطر	mushrooms
fool Soya	فول صويا	soybeans
fool sudaaneyy	فول سوداني	peanuts
gambaree	جمبري	shrimp (prawns)
ganzabeel	جنزبيل	ginger
Hamaam	حمام	pigeon
jazar	جزر	carrot

I'm allergic

to seafood!

kalaawi	كلاوي	kidney
khiyaar	خيار	cucumber
kibda	كبدة	liver
laHm baqareyy	لحم بقري	beef
laHm bitel-lo	لحم بتلو	veal
laHm maa'iz	لحم ماعز	goat
laimoon	ليمون	lemon
ma'koolaat baHrey-ya	مأكولات بحرية	seafood
mawz	موز	banana
mekas-saraat	مكسرات	nuts
samak	سمك	fish
shaT-Ta	شطة	chili
TamaaTim	طماطم	tomato
thawm	ثوم	garlic
tof-faaH	تفاح	apple
za'tar	زعتر	thyme
dora	ذرة	corn

to seafood!

Stop,

KEY WORDS

I've been robbed!	سرقوني ◊	saraqoonee
thief	حرامي ◊	Haraameyy
robbery	سرقة ◊	sariqa
pick-pocket	نشال ◊	nash-shaal
police	شرطة ◊	shorTa
(police) station	القسم ◊	al-qism
(police) report	محضر ◊	maHDar
form	استمارة ◊	istimaara
insurance	تأمين ◊	ta'meen
suitcase	حقيبة سفر ◊ Haqeebat safar	
hand bag	حقيبة يد ◊ Haqeebat yad	
briefcase	حقيبة عمل ◊ Haqeebat 'amal	

Stop

thief!

camera	كاميرا ◆ *kamera*
car trunk (boot)	شنطة السيارة ◆ *shonTat as-say-yaara*
cell phone (mobile phone)	محمول ◆ *maHmool*
computer	كمبيوتر ◆ *kombyootir*
earrings	حلق ◆ *Halaq*
ring	خاتم ◆ *khaatim*
necklace	عقد ◆ *'uqd*
bracelet	سوار ◆ *suwaar*
gold	ذهب ◆ *dahab*
diamond	الماس ◆ *al-maas*
watch	ساعة ◆ *saa'a*
passport	جواز سفر ◆ *jawaaz safar*

thief!

I want to report a theft	أريد أن أبلغ عن سرقة ◇ *oreed an ubal-ligh 'an sariqa*
I've lost...	...فقدت ◇ *faqadt*
I was attacked	هجموا علي ◇ *hajamoo 'aleyy*
I had put it in my bag	وضعتها في حقيبتي ◇ *waDa'tuhaa fee Haqeebatee*
It was taken from my pocket	أخذوها من جيبي ◇ *akhazoohaa min jaibee*
I left it in my room	تركتها في غرفتي ◇ *taraktoohaa fee ghorfatee*
This happened today	هذا حدث اليوم ◇ *haaza Hadath al-yawm*

thief!

It happened yesterday	هذا حدث أمس
	◆ *haaza Hadath ams*
I need a copy of the police report	أحتاج صورة من المحضر
	◆ *aHtaaj Soora min al-maHDar*

⚡TAKE NOTE⚡

Travelers in the Middle East have traditionally enjoyed 'honored guest' status. This probably has its roots in trips that lasted months on camel-back through deserts.

According to a religious and cultural code a 'passer-by' is entitled to certain privileges that used to include shelter, and today still do include protection and safe passage. If you think it's bad news for you to have something stolen, be sure it's a lot worse news for the thief if he gets caught.

A sure way of ruining your trip is losing or misplacing an important item. Most people will head straight for their consulates, but sometimes this is not possible and they have to report the incident to the local police.

thief!

DESCRIBING ITEMS

new	جديد ◆ *jadeed*
old	قديم ◆ *qadeem*
big	كبير ◆ *kabeer*
small	صغير ◆ *Sagheer*
black	أسود ◆ *aswad*
blue	أزرق ◆ *azraq*
brown	بني ◆ *bon-nee*
green	أخضر ◆ *akhDar*
orange	برتقالي ◆ *bortoqaalee*
pink	وردي ◆ *wardee*
purple	بنفسجي ◆ *banafsajee*
red	أحمر ◆ *aHmar*
white	أبيض ◆ *abyaD*
yellow	أصفر ◆ *aSfar*

thief!

leather	جلد ◇ *jild*
valuable	قيم ◇ *qay-yim*
immitation	تقليد ◇ *taqleed*
authentic	أصلي ◇ *aSlee*
antique	تحفة ◇ *toHfa*

أشر هنا من فضلك ... please point here

ماذا فقدت؟	What's missing?
ما لونه؟	What color was it?
ما قيمته؟	How much was it worth?
هل اسمك عليه؟	Did it have your name on it?

أشر هنا من فضلك ... please point here

thief!

DESCRIBING PEOPLE

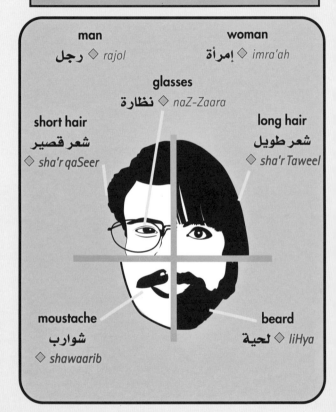

man	woman
◇ *rajol* رجل	◇ *imra'ah* إمرأة

glasses
◇ *naZ-Zaara* نظارة

short hair
شعر قصير
◇ *sha'r qaSeer*

long hair
شعر طويل
◇ *sha'r Taweel*

moustache
شوارب
◇ *shawaarib*

beard
◇ *liHya* لحية

about ... years old   حوالي...عاما
◇ *Hawaaleyy...'aaman*

Stop,

thief!

tall	◆ طويل Taweel
short	◆ قصير qaSeer
fat	◆ سمين sameen
thin	◆ نحيل naHeel
old	◆ مسن mos-sinn
young	◆ شاب shaabb

please point here ... أشر هنا من فضلك ..

املأ هذه الاستمارة	Fill out this form
وقع هنا	Sign here
سننظر في الأمر	We'll look into it
وجدناها!	We've found it!
سأحضر شخصا يتكلم الانجليزية	I'll get someone who speaks English
مسؤول الأمن سيتولى الموضوع	The security officer will deal with it

please point here ...

thief!

KEY WORDS

arrested	مقبوض عليه ◇ *maqbooD 'alaih*
attorney (lawyer)	محام ◇ *moHaami*
bail	كفالة ◇ *kafaala*
charge	تهمة ◇ *tohma*
consulate	قنصلية ◇ *qonSoley-ya*
court	محكمة ◇ *maHkama*
defense	دفاع ◇ *difaa'*
deportation	ترحيل ◇ *tarHeel*
embassy	سفارة ◇ *sifaara*
fine	غرامة ◇ *gharaama*
interpreter	مترجم ◇ *motarjim*
judge	قاض ◇ *qaaDee*
law	قانون ◇ *qaanoon*

legal	قانوني ◈ *qanooneyy*
(police) officer	ضابط ◈ *Daabit*
(police) station	قسم ◈ *qism*
prison	سجن ◈ *sijn*
prosecution	إدعاء ◈ *id-di'aa'*
statement	أقوال ◈ *aqwaal*
suspect	متهم ◈ *mot-taham*
warning	إنذار ◈ *inzaar*
possession	حيازة ◈ *Hiyaaza*
smuggling	تهريب ◈ *tahreeb*
narcotics	مخدرات ◈ *mokhad-diraat*
stolen goods	بضائع مسروقة ◈ *baDaa'i masrooqa*

⚡ TAKE NOTE ⚡

The idea of being a "guest" has obligations as well as privilages. Subtle signals can relay that you are trying to be considerate towards the culture and mindful of people's sensitivities. Observe a modest dress code, avoid flaunting wealth, and rein in any amorous impulses in public. That should endear you to most.

I apologise	أنا آسف ◇ *anaa aasif*
I'm just visiting	أنا زائر ◇ *anaa zaa'ir*
It wasn't me	ليس أنا ◇ *laisa ana*
I don't understand	لا أفهم ◇ *laa afham*
I can't read this	لا أستطيع أن أقرأ هذا ◇ *laa astaTee' an* *aqra' haaza*
I didn't know it's forbiddden	لم أكن أعرف أنه ممنوع ◇ *lam akon aa'rif* *an-nuh mamnoo'*
Is he under arrest?	هل هو مقبوض عليه؟ ◇ *hal huwa maqbooD 'alaih*

Do we need to remove our shoes?	هل نخلع الأحذية؟ ◇ *hal nakhla' al-aHzeya*
Are they fasting?	هل هم صائمين؟ ◇ *hal hom Saa'meen*
Are these clothes suitable?	هل هذه الملابس مناسبة؟ ◇ *hal haazihil malaabis monaasiba*

أشر هنا من فضلك ... please point here

هذا غير قانوني	That's illegal
سأعطيك إنذار هذه المرة	I'll just warn you this time
يجب أن تدفع الغرامة	You have to pay the fine
أين جواز سفرك؟	Where's your passport?
يجب أن تأتي معي إلى القسم	You have to come with me to the station

please point here ... أشر هنا من فضلك ...

Keeping out

Can I call the ...	ممكن اتصل... ◈ *momkin at-taSil*
American embassy?	بسفارة أمريكا ◈ *bi-sifaarit amreeka*
British embassy?	بسفارة بريطانيا ◈ *bi sifaarit biriTanya*
Canadian consulate?	قنصلية كندا ◈ *qonSoley-yat kanada*
I need an English-speaking lawyer	أريد محام يتكلم انجليزي ◈ *oreed moHaami yetkal-lam ingeleezeyy*
I have to contact my family	يجب أن أتصل بأسرتي ◈ *yajib an at-taSil bi'osratee*
I need to make a phone call	أريد أن أتصل بالتليفون ◈ *oreed an at-taSil bit-tilifoon*
I don't know anything about it	لا أعرف عنه شيء ◈ *laa 'araf 'anuh shai'*

I can't say anything yet

لا أقدر أن أقول شيئا الآن
◆ *laa aqdar an aqool shai'an al-aan*

هل لديك أقوال؟	Do you want to make a statement?
هل تريد أن تتصل بالتليفون؟	Do you want to make a phone call?
هذه حقوقك	These are your rights
المترجم سيأتي الآن	The interpreter is coming now
أسرتك هنا	Your family is here
لا تخافوا، أنتم في أمان هنا	Don't be afraid, you're safe here

please point here ...

What are you charging me with?	ما هي تهمتي؟ ◇ *maa hiya tohmati*
How much is the fine?	كم الغرامة؟ ◇ *kam al gharaama*
Can I post bail?	ممكن أدفع كفالة؟ ◇ *momkin adfa' kafaala*

# of trouble

Will I stand trial?   هل ستحاكموني؟
◆ *hal sa-toHaakimoonee*

How long do I have to stay here?   إلى متى سأظل هنا؟
◆ *ilaa mataa saZall huna*

لن نتهمك بشئ	We won't be charging you
تفضل، مع السلامة	You're free to go
يجب أن تعود إلينا	You need to come back
اترك جواز سفرك	Leave your passport
نريدك أن ترد على بعض الأسئلة	We want you to answer some questions

73

NUMBERS

one	واحد ◇ *waaHid*	
two	اثنان ◇ *ithnaan*	
three	ثلاثة ◇ *thalaatha*	
four	أربعة ◇ *arba'a*	
five	خمسة ◇ *khamsa*	
six	ستة ◇ *sit-ta*	
seven	سبعة ◇ *sab'a*	
eight	ثمانية ◇ *thamanya*	
nine	تسعة ◇ *tis'a*	
ten	عشرة ◇ *'ashra*	
eleven	إحدى عشر ◇ *iHda 'ashar*	
twelve	اثنا عشر ◇ *ithna 'ashar*	
thirteen	ثلاثة عشر ◇ *thalaath 'ashar*	
fourteen	أربعة عشر ◇ *arba'at 'ashar*	
fifteen	خمسة عشر ◇ *khamsat 'ashar*	
sixteen	ستة عشر ◇ *sit-tat 'ashar*	
seventeen	سبعة عشر ◇ *sab'at 'ashar*	
eighteen	ثمانية عشر ◇ *thamaniyat 'ashar*	
nineteen	تسعة عشر ◇ *tis'at 'ashar*	

Quick

reference

twenty	عشرين ◊ *'ishreen*
twenty-one	**واحد وعشرين** ◊ *waaHid wa 'ishreen*
twenty-two	**اثنان وعشرين** ◊ *ithnaan wa 'ishreen*
thirty	ثلاثين ◊ *thalaatheen*
forty	أربعين ◊ *arba'een*
fifty	خمسين ◊ *khamseen*
sixty	ستين ◊ *sitteen*
seventy	سبعين ◊ *sab'een*
eighty	ثمانين ◊ *thamaneen*
ninety	تسعين ◊ *tis'een*
one hundred	مئة ◊ *mi'a*
one thousand	ألف ◊ *alf*

> ⚡ **TAKE NOTE** ⚡
>
> Although you will find western numbers used in the Middle East, Arabic also has its own set of figures:
>
> | ٠ | ١ | ٢ | ٣ | ٤ | ٥ | ٦ | ٧ | ٨ | ٩ |
> |---|---|---|---|---|---|---|---|---|---|
> | 0 | 1 | 2 | 3 | 4 | 5 | 6 | 7 | 8 | 9 |

What's the time?
كم الساعة؟
◇ *kam as-saa'a*

It's two o'clock
الساعة اثنين
◇ *as-saa'a ithnain*

`11:00`
الساعة إحدى عشرة
◇ *as-saa'a iHda 'ashar*

`11:15`
الساعة إحدى عشرة وربع
◇ *as-saa'a ithna 'ashar*

`14:30`
اثنين ونصف
◇ *ithnain wa niSf*

`14:45`
ثلاثة إلا ربع
◇ *thalaatha il-la rub'*

Monday	الأثنين ◆ al-ithnain
Tuesday	الثلاثاء ◆ ath-thulaathaa'
Wednesday	الأربعاء ◆ al-arbi'aa'
Thursday	الخميس ◆ al-khamees
Friday	الجمعة ◆ aj-jum'a
Saturday	السبت ◆ as-sabt
Sunday	الأحد ◆ al-aHad
now	الآن ◆ al-aan
soon	قريبا ◆ qareeban
today	اليوم ◆ al-yawm
yesterday	أمس ◆ ams
tomorrow	غدا ◆ ghadan

MONTHS

English	Arabic	Transliteration
January	يناير	◈ *yanaayir*
February	فبراير	◈ *febraayir*
March	مارس	◈ *maaris*
April	أبريل	◈ *abreel*
May	مايو	◈ *maayo*
June	يونيو	◈ *yoonyo*
July	يوليو	◈ *yoolyo*
August	أغسطس	◈ *aghostos*
September	سبتمبر	◈ *sibtimbir*
October	أكتوبر	◈ *octobir*
November	نوفمبر	◈ *novimbir*
December	ديسمبر	◈ *deesimbir*
What's today's date?	ما هو تاريخ اليوم؟	◈ *maa huwa tareekh al-yawm*
It's June 12	١٢ يونيو	◈ *ithna 'ashar yoonyo*

Quick

SIGNS

ENTRANCE
دخول
dokhool

DANGER
خطر
khaTar

EXIT
خروج
khorooj

MEN
رجال
rijaal

WOMEN
سيدات
sayyidaat

RESTROOMS
دورات مياه
dawraat miyaah

NO ENTRY
الدخول ممنوع
ad-dokhool mamnoo

NO SMOKING
التدخين ممنوع
mamnoo' at-tadkheen

ISBN 1-903103-10-X

For information, address:
g-and-w publishing
47A High Street
Chinnor
Oxfordshire
OX39 4DJ
www.g-and-w.co.uk

Designed by Upfront Creative, London, UK
www.upfrontcreative.com

Printed in Hong Kong

03 04 05 06 07 08   12 11 10 9 8 7 6 5 4 3 2 1